What Freemasonry Means to Me
Volume 2

What Freemasonry Means to Me

What Freemasonry Means to Me
Volume 2

Edited and Compiled by
Daryl Lamar Andrews

What Freemasonry Means to Me
Volume 2

Edited and Compiled by Daryl Lamar Andrews
Prince Hall Masonic Journal

Copyright by
Most Worshipful Prince Hall Grand Lodge
Free & Accepted Masons
State of Illinois and Its Jurisdiction, 2017

Published in 2017
by
Most Worshipful Prince Hall Grand Lodge
Free & Accepted Masons
State of Illinois and Its Jurisdiction

Contents

Table of Contents	Page
Dedication	*i*
Acknowledgements	*ii*
Foreword	*iii*
Duty and Peace *by Benjamin Franklin Rogers*	*1*
Diamond to a Square *by Edward Briscoe*	*9*
Tasks of the Heaven Bound *by Alexander A. Martin*	*15*
Membership: Many Things *by Reginald F. Foster*	*21*
Brotherhood of Man *by Dr. John C. Ellis*	*27*
Darkness to Light *by Brian Beatty*	*33*
Masonry and Progress *by Ashby B. Carter*	*39*
Power to Unite *by Eric Harrell*	*45*
Teaches Men How to Live *by James H. Black Sr.*	*49*

Dedication

Freemasonry is a progressive science and this work is dedicated to those progressive giants of the past, the present and the future who have worked, are currently working and will, eventually work to improve the state of society and the world.

It is also dedicated to the memory of the first leaders of Illinois Prince Hall Masons, namely, Harrison D. King, Chairman of the convention to form the Illinois Grand Lodge; Benjamin Franklin Rogers, first Grand Master; John Jones, Grand Master of Ohio Prince Hall Masons; and to the other founding fathers who drove the organization.

Acknowledgements

The "What Freemasonry Means to Me" project is sponsored by the Prince Hall Masonic Journal which is the official publication of the Most Worshipful Prince Hall Grand Lodge of Illinois.

Special acknowledgements are due to Most Worshipful Brother Dwayne A. Smith, Grand Master of Illinois Prince Hall Masons; Right Worshipful Brother Aubrey K. Barlow, Deputy Grand Master; The Brian L. Abrams Chapter of the Phylaxis Society; and the all of the individual Masons who have submitted their essays and articles in Volume One and Volume Two.

Foreword

History is the backbone of who we are. This is a statement that has been uttered through multiple channels from multiple mouths because it is the ultimate truth. Freemasonry has a long and colorful history which includes ups and downs. Yet, despite the shifts of the tides, the tenets of the organization have remained the same and have not wavered through the years.

This is, most likely, the reason why the meaning of Freemasonry to individual Masons has also remained consistent over the years. To many, the fraternity served and continues to serve as a beacon of light in times of darkness. To many, the Masonic emblem is a signal light which identifies the man who wears it as a credible individual with morals. To many, it is a way of life which embodies both of the aforementioned points. But, it's consistency over the years in providing service to those who need it most, yields similar feelings on the meaning of Freemasonry by many men and has done so for years.

Volume Two of What Freemasonry Means to Me provides a mixture of commentary from Masons of the past to Masons of the current era in honor of the one hundred fiftieth year of existence of the Most Worshipful Prince Hall Grand Lodge of Illinois. Excerpts of addresses from leaders of the Masonic Order that live in past Masonic Proceedings and articles from publications of the Prince Hall Masonic Journal and Past Masters Topics magazines are being brought to light for the first time in a number of years. In addition, submissions by brethren from the current era are being brought to light. Thus, giving a mixture of perspectives from across the eras. Although the themes of each of the submissions are similar in nature, they provide insight on the meaning of Freemasonry from different perspectives which adds to the importance of this work.

With thousands of Prince Hall Freemasons in the State of Illinois who are active in multiple capacities today, it is expected for these sentiments to remain similar in future volumes of this series. This can be stated with great confidence because the values that are espoused by the Masonic Order which were executed by the brethren of the past are still intact and being executed by the brethren of today. Individual Masons are active at multiple levels within their communities providing relief to those in need and providing truth in areas of darkness. These, ultimately, define the concept of brotherly love because we all believe that we, as human beings, are brothers under the fatherhood of God. It is with this in mind, that I look forward to future volumes on the subject of "What Freemasonry Means to Me" to hear more perspectives on the subject from Prince Hall Masons not only in Illinois but also across the globe.

Daryl Lamar Andrews
Editor
Prince Hall Masonic Journal

Duty

and Peace

Most Worshipful Brother
Benjamin Franklin Rogers
Grand Master
Prince Hall Grand Lodge of Illinois
1867 - 1869, 1873 – 1877
Central Lodge #3

What Freemasonry Means to Me

Brethren, by the wisdom of the Supreme Architect of the universe and your suffrages, I have been called to preside as Grand Master over the First Grand Lodge of Colored Masons for the State of Illinois, and had I not confidence in the ability of my brother officers, I feel that I should shrink from duty; but knowing their ability I shall, under God, endeavor to do my duty to the best of my judgment.

Therefore, Brethren, let us at the commencement of our session give thanks to the Giver of all good for the many blessings and comforts which He is daily and hourly bestowing upon us, and in our deliberations through this session, may we constantly look up to him, and may he endow us with wisdom, patience and brotherly love. Not having any official acts to communicate to this Grand body since my installation into office, I shall take pleasure in saying something to the craft, which I hope will be elevating in its nature, and inspire the brethren to perform every known duty, and live close to the principles of Masonry.

What Freemasonry Means to Me

Brethren, in view of the origin and true nature of the institution of Masonry, its high importance to the world, the sacredness of its principles, its harmonizing influences, and the whole excellence of the system, whether it be considered in a historical, benevolent, moral, or religious point, your minds must be solemnly affected, and your hearts seriously engaged, to maintain the purity of its precepts, not only as a plain and reasonable duty, but as examples waiting to be imitated by those who shall receive the administration from your hands.

Brethren, your profession is built upon a tried foundation; you stand solemnly pledged to the world to maintain the cause of truth against all the assaults of vice, or the inroads of error. Your several lodges are, or ought to be, so many temples of virtue, and schools of moral and religious instruction; each individual should be a watchful sentinel over the happiness of mankind, ever on the alert to rescue injured innocence, or to avert impending dangers. Such, however, is the state of the world, and such the unhappy lot of all institutions, that none have been free from the unhallowed tread of unworthy members. Even in thy little family, O, Blessed Immanuel, was there a betraying Judas! Nor is thy sacred table always surrounded by sanctified hearts. This is greatly to be lamented, yet from the nature of man it cannot be wholly prevented in our present state: much however, may be done to remedy this general evil. Let it therefore be remembered and written as with sunbeams on the heart of every Mason, that the harmony and happiness of your assemblies, and your true enjoyment as individuals, does not, cannot depend upon your numbers, but on the real intrinsic worth, the virtue, the integrity and the moral excellence of your members; this is a great point as respects the unity and fellowship of Masonic Brethren.

You are, therefore, to make a full and thorough examination as to the true character of those who may present themselves, for the benefit of our order. That is a point never to be left unguarded; all the internal social friendship and happiness of your communications vitally depend upon it: let the world know assuredly, that if any individual desires admission to your privileges, that the square of justice and the plumb line of rectitude must fit his character for that important place; let it be well-understood that vice is not to be winked at, that the doors of your lodges can never be opened for the reception of a doubtful character; that the sanctity of the institutions is not to be trampled underfoot by the profane, that the precepts of Masonry present an insurmountable barrier against every immoral person; hence the effect would be of great consequence to yourselves, even in a private capacity, to the reputation of your lodge, as a wise institution, and to the general good of mankind as a standard and a rallying point for virtue. The pure, pious, and meritorious part of the community, many of whom now stand aloof, would crowd your assemblies; then might you enjoy more abundant social friendship in your stated communications, and the world in view of your regular tenets and increasing respectability be more deeply affected with the general utility of Masonry. However, should an unworthy person gain admission within the veils of your sanctum, remember something ought immediately to be done; adopt all probable and proper means to mend his heart, change his habits and establish his good character; persuade him to practice virtue from the love of it.

In relation to Masonic discipline, we all know that it is too remiss. Members are sometimes allowed to transgress the laws and pass with impunity. Each brother excuses himself on the ground that it will be more proper, or that it will be attended with more salutary consequences, for some other brother to enter complaint; in this way it is sometimes finally neglected, so that what is every man's duty, is eventually performed by none. Brothers, purge your Lodges of bad men; do your duty to the brotherhood; better, by far, that a limb be amputated, than to have the whole body affected with its poisonous matter. Do not fail to use the black ball in cases of necessity.

Temperance is one of the cardinal virtues of our order; but, I am pained to say to you, my brethren, that I have met intemperance in places where of all other it ought not to be. Do you look for virtue, morality, and brotherly love, to emanate from one of those sinks of iniquity? As well might you expect to pick "figs from thistles;" and when one of our number becomes so depraved, and all means have been exhausted to reclaim him, and he cannot be saved, do your duty by making him an example for other evil-doers.

Finally, brethren, let us keep the unity of the spirit in the bonds of peace. Let us love one another, for love is God. "Behold! How good and pleasant it is for brethren to dwell together in unity. It is like the precious ointment upon the head that ran down upon the beard, even --- Aaron's beard, that went down to the skirts of his garment. As the dew of Herman, and as the dew that descended upon the mountains of Zion, for there the Lord commanded the blessing, even life forever more."

Source: Rogers, Benjamin Franklin., "First Annual Address", Proceedings, MWPHGL of Illinois, 1867

About Grand Master Rogers

Benjamin Franklin Rogers, the very first Grand Master of Illinois Prince Hall Masons from 1867 to 1869, was an abolitionist and a noted civil rights activist in Central Illinois. His efforts in the City of Springfield, Illinois and surrounding areas helped to ensure freedom for those who escaped the bondages of Slavery and an education for African American children within the vicinity. Having been selected as the very first Leader of a Grand Lodge of Masons, his leadership ability was stellar. The evidence of which is also shown in his selection, again, to the Office of Grand Master from 1873 through 1877.

Diamond
to a Square

Brother Edward Briscoe
Cornerstone Lodge #91

As a child who was reared in the third largest metropolitan city in the country, I was exposed to many opportunities that yielded robust experiences. Of them, none provided a more rewarding life lesson than that of joining my local Boys of America Scout troop # 778.

Though I did not want to participate at first I was fortunate enough to have an active father and other positive male influences that instilled in me the ideology of privilege that membership in this type of group would hold for me then and now. They were speaking of the tangible and intangible lessons that would propel my personal character to another level amongst my peers.

Upon completing scouting at the highest rank of Eagle Scout, I finally began to take heed in the lessons of my father and other men when they said "membership has its privileges". As a young man entering college I grew an unquenchable thirst for opportunities that would allow me to further shape, among other things, my moral fortitude, academic intellect and social aptitude just as scouting had given me. To meet that desire, on April 21, 2005 I was initiated in the Nashville Alumni Chapter of Kappa Alpha Psi Fraternity, Inc. In the great noble klan of Kappa I was further indoctrinated with knowledge of true manhood which is explained in the pledge process and throughout the ongoing business of the fraternity.

One of the symbolic representations that Kappa impressed upon me was the diamond. Like a true God fearing man who is unbreakable, so is a diamond. It is the hardest substance known to mankind. Many great men, particularly those we read about in the annals of history, knew this to be their truth. I am cohesively linked to these men and their contributions to humanity through the bond of Kappa. Again, membership has privileges, tangible and intangible.

Entering adulthood with an unwavering commitment to continue aligning myself with like-minded men-men who place value in family, community, and self-awareness, I sought direction from men who I saw practicing this. These men were educators, spiritual leaders and skilled tradesmen who I had come to know throughout my life. While each carried a unique perspective on life and its ills, they all shared a common thread - Prince Hall Freemasonry. This served as my catalyst of interest in the fraternity and led my exploration into seeking "the light".

On Saturday, May 11, 2013, I was raised to the third degree of Prince Hall Freemasonry in Cornerstone Lodge #91 of Chicago, Illinois. It is a life fulfilling opportunity to be an active member of an age-old organization that was founded by a single man of color and is internationally accepted and respected.

As a Prince Hall Mason, I reap the benefits of membership through ritualistic teachings of the degrees. I'm afforded time and candid conversations with accomplished men in all fields of human endeavor. Alongside my fellow brother mason, I feel equal in a polarized world that often times negatively categories African American men.

As a Master Mason, I am better equipped to serve God, my family, and the surrounding community; in that order. When I pass the token of a grip to a Mason, I know that I am meeting a man who seeks a better life for not just himself but for all mankind. This, in part with the foundational upbringing I have shapes my understanding of what it means to be a Freemason.

What Freemasonry Means to Me

Tasks of the

Heaven-bound

Most Worshipful Brother
Alexander A. Martin
Grand Master
Prince Hall Grand Lodge of Illinois
1913 - 1919
Ionic Lodge #46

All true Masons are heaven bound. To be a Mason is to live in accordance with and in obedience to, the second great commandment, as proclaimed by God in the holy writ - "Though shalt love thy neighbor as thy self."

Prince Hall Masons have dedicated themselves to establishment of this commandment on earth, and the doctrine of the Fatherhood of God and the Brotherhood of man. The world may grow wise in science, transportation and a thousand new ways to increase the world's riches, yet the opportunity for happiness remains in the field of brotherly love. Remembering that the law of life is a law of strife and only through painful efforts, energy and determined courage, can we move on to better things, Brotherhood still remains a task. The time has come for us, as Prince Hall Masons to assume a more active leadership in carrying out the task of Brotherhood.

Most of the great problems facing our country today are only larger aspects of the evil passions that Masonry is trying to subdue. We firmly believe that all our brothers who have passed on since last we met are now reposing in the arms of the All in All. Nothing we can do here, or say here, can console them now. They are far beyond the realm of consolation. They, very truly, exemplified the spirit of our fraternity; to help the needy, to succor the distressed and support everything that is fine and noble. Their lives were epitomes of courage, vision and deep faith --- an example worthy of emulation by all who love their fellowman. What we do here and say here, is for the living; those of us who are left here and for those who are to come after them and after us. After all, what do we ask of life here, or hereafter, but the privilege to serve, to live, to commune with our fellowman, and from the lap of the earth to look up into the face of God.

Our departed brothers have played their part in the arena of Masonry. They have been a credit to the memory of the immortal Prince Hall. They have left footprints on the sands of fellowship, and their illustrious memory shall course down the corridors of time. Veneration of the past is honorable and desirable, respect for traditions and ancient customs is good, to study old things is helpful to understanding, but Masons are builders in an unfinished world and all the past is but a challenge to us as Prince Hall Masons.

It is the goal of every Prince Hall Mason to create an unobstructed law of the universe, administered by justice, wisdom and mercy; a law of balance, of beauty, of spiritual harmony, to promote faith which is the reality of Divine promise, and to project love. How could we forget the men who have helped to carry the banner of this mighty host of consecrated men to the topmost round of the ladder? We shall not, we cannot! By reason of the fortitude of men like these, Prince Hall Masonry has gone on unabated down through the years, while countless other fraternal organizations have folded and been forgotten.

Now let us go forth resolved that their lives have not been in vain: that the high principles which actuated them shall henceforth have an uplifting influence upon us, so that the good which they did may endure forever.

Source: Martin, Alexander A., Excerpt from Annual Address, Proceedings, MWPHGL of Illinois, 1913

About Grand Master Martin

Alexander A. Martin of Cairo, Illinois served as the sixteenth Grand Master of Illinois Prince Hall Masons from 1913 to 1919. Martin served as Grand Master while the United States of America was embroiled in World War One. Serving at the helm of Illinois Prince Hall Masons throughout the term of the war, he executed the duties of his office efficiently guiding the Grand Lodge with a firm hand to stability.

What Freemasonry Means to Me

Membership:

Many Things

Brother Reginald F. Foster
Silver Square Lodge #62

Membership in the brotherhood of Masons means many things. Away from home to attend Alabama A&M University. I roomed with three other young men from Birmingham, Alabama. They were Masons from the Prince Hall Affiliated Lodge #410 of the Jurisdiction of Alabama. I didn't know anything about this fraternity and wanted to become a member. On October 19, 1985 I was raised a member of this great fraternity.

To me, it means being part of an unbroken tradition that stretches back over 225 years to a time when guilds of Prince Hall Masons traveled throughout Massachusetts laying the stones of the great first Black Masonic Lodges of the Prince Hall Grand Lodge of Massachusetts.

Being a free black man and showing manhood, I believe Prince Hall was interested in the Masonic fraternity because Freemasonry was founded upon the ideals of liberty, equality and peace. Prior to the American Revolutionary War, Prince Hall and fourteen other free black men petitioned for admittance to the white Boston St. John's Lodge. They were turned down. Having been rejected by colonial Freemasonry, Hall and 14 others never gave up. They persevered and were initiated into Masonry by members claiming to be of Lodge No. 441 of the Grand Lodge of Ireland on March 6, 1775 which was attached to the British forces stationed in Boston. Eventually, Hall and other freedmen founded African Lodge, later African Grand Lodge and Hall was named Grand Master. Prince Hall is recognized by many as the Father of Black Masonry in the United States. Historically, many believe he made it possible for Negroes to be recognized and enjoy all privileges of Free and Accepted Masonry.

This experience showed me that I too can be successful and persevere. I was once a poor, free black man who grew up against all odds in the ghetto streets of the Eastside of Chicago Heights, Illinois in the 1960s, 1970s and the 1980s. I was also raised by a single parent. Against all odds, I persevered.

Furthermore, through Freemasonry, I have had the opportunity to break bread with good men, some of whom belong to faiths other than my own Christian faith. Freemasonry is, for all its members, a supplement to good living which has enhanced the lives of millions who have entered its doors. Though it is not a religion, it supplements faith in God the Creator. It is indeed supporting of morality and virtue.

Freemasonry is built upon three basic tenants - Brotherly Love, Relief and Truth. Brotherly Love is the practice of the Golden Rule. Relief embodies charity for all mankind. Truth is honesty, fair play and adherence to the cardinal virtues. These moral lessons are taught during three ceremonies, or "degrees" through allegory and symbolism using the traditional stonemason's tools. Of all of the cardinal virtues, none is more valued in Masonry than selfless giving. Examples of Masonic charity are legendary.

Freemasonry is much more than a social organization. Through Masonic teachings, good men practice love and charity. As a caring Fraternity for humanity, Black Masons spend millions of dollars to support the less fortunate. For a person to have the opportunity to become whole and productive is, to me, exciting and wonderful. This opportunity is given at no cost to his or her family or the state.

Living is beautiful but sometimes life can be harsh and cruel. Whenever or wherever people are in need Masons are there to help. From large undertakings to the smallest of needs, Masons are always there, caring and serving.

It is also beautiful having Friends Wherever you go. Because of this, members can find brother Masons wherever they go. Across the country and around the world, there are Lodges in virtually every city and many smaller communities. It is a good feeling to know that wherever a man's travels may take him, he has friends that he can depend on and trust.

To me, Freemasonry is one form of dedication to God and service to humanity. It is in my heart and, so, I will remain. I am proud of my involvement. I am proud to walk in fraternal fellowship with my Brethren. Why am I a Freemason? Simply because I am proud to be a man who wants to keep the moral standards of life at high level and leave something behind so others will benefit. Only as I, personally, become better, can I help others to do the same.

What Freemasonry Means to Me

Brotherhood

of Friends

Most Worshipful Brother
Dr. John C. Ellis
Grand Master
Prince Hall Grand Lodge of Illinois
1924 – 1944
Decatur (John C. Ellis) Lodge #17

Masonry teaches the brotherhood of man. There can be no true brotherhood of man without true friendship. What is a friend? He is a person with whom you dare to be yourself. He asks of you to assume nothing, hide nothing, only to be what you are. You do not have to be on your guard. You can say what you think, express what you feel. With him you breathe freely. You can take off your coat and loosen your collar. You can reveal your little vanities and your absurd hobbies, your likes and dislikes, and in disclosing them to him, they are lost and swallowed up in the ocean of his loyalty.

A friend is not to be our echo. He comes nearest to us because he is other than our self. There have been one-sided friendships in which the more self-forgetting partner merely supplemented the happiness and gifts of his friend but that is to have been a clinging parasite rather than a completing and inspiring companion.

With a friend you do not have to be careful. He understands. He is like fire that purifies all you do. He is like water that cleanses all you say. He is like wine that warms you to the bone. In true friendship there must be both give and take. Patience and forbearance, rather than blindness to faults and failings, are its essential characteristics. We should not ask too much if we expect to keep friendships and, most of all, we must be ready to give ourselves at our very best to meet all the needs and expectations of our friends. Friendship is to mankind the most precious possession, a thing infinite and immortal which improves happiness, abates misery, and divides sorrow. Love is the image of God, and not a lifeless image, but the living essence of the divine nature.

Truth is the foundation of all knowledge and the cement of all societies, the property of no individual, but the treasure of all men. Friendship, love, and truth - these are the three bright stars that shed their divine radiance over the dark ocean of human existence. Without their guidance, earth would be no more than a prison pen from which we would long to escape to other homes, and the soul of man would remain forever a brother to the clod.

In the exaltation of these principles, our order has found its greatest hold upon the hearts of men. Masonry has become one of the most powerful agencies in the combat with ignorance, vice, intolerance, bigotry and the host of evils that beset mankind at every step of its earthly career. Masonry exists in response to the cravings of the human soul for a domain of brotherhood, a fraternity wherein sweet and congenial companionship and mutual offices of kindness may soften the rigors of existence and give mankind a foretaste of the life beyond.

Source: Ellis, Dr. John C., Excerpt from Annual Address, Proceedings, MWPHGL of Illinois, 1938, p.12-13

About Grand Master Ellis

Dr. John C. Ellis, a dentist by profession, served as the eighteenth Grand Master of Illinois Prince Hall Masons from 1924 to 1944. He holds the distinction of being the longest serving Grand Master of Illinois Prince Hall Masons in the history of the organization. Through his steady and competent hands of leadership, the Grand Lodge survived challenges presented during the Great Depression and World War Two. His efforts during a period where other organizations were unable to sustain themselves through the challenges of the era were, simply, extraordinary.

Darkness

to Light

Brother Brian Beatty
Mt. Moriah Lodge #28

This one statement has ruled my life as a Mason - "From Darkness Comes Light" - and it is how I have tried to walk as a Master Mason. Knowing that I, just as every other Mason, who has encountered that statement, find that it was the basis and start of a wonderful journey. We move from our darkness to the light of Masonry. I try to instill that emphasis in everyone I help to enlighten in the Craft being one who had the uniqueness of moving between two different forms of Masonry.

To have been raised in an Ancient Free and Accepted Mason Military Lodge to being brought over to a Prince Hall Free and Accepted Mason Lodge is a gift. I know that I am not the only one, but in the Prince Hall Family, we are not the majority. I have walked on both sides and must say that I like this side more.

There is a special meaning to being able to call myself a Prince Hall Mason. I moved from the darkness of my heritage to the light of being a Master Mason in the Prince Hall Fraternity. The knowledge that I have obtained has worked wonders in my Masonic life. I am more active in my Lodge and the entire organization than I ever was when I was a non-Prince Hall Mason. My activity level increased because my eyes had been opened to this reality.

There, I was just a "meeting" Mason, and when I moved on from Oklahoma, I didn't move on with my Masonic walk. I guess I knew that something was missing and, as I met Prince Hall Brothers, I began to find what I never knew about our walk. The first time I went in with no former knowledge, but this time, I went in knowing that I would receive the parts of my Masonic life that were missing. The blindfold was now off and the veil had been lifted when they said to me "Let there be Light and there was Light."

I can truly say that for the first time in my life, that statement was completely true. I will forever be grateful to the Brothers of Mount Moriah Lodge No.28 for accepting me into their Lodge and making me a Prince Hall Master Mason. I know that the past, the present, and as we move into the future, that the foundation is solid and sound. For anyone I meet or have a part in influencing, I hope that I can impart to them some of the Light that has been imprinted on me.

What Freemasonry Means to Me

For years, Freemasonry was just something I had done, but now, it is my walk, talk, mannerisms, heart, life, soul and mind. I am in every Male House in Masonry and two Female Houses whereas, before, I was just a Lodge member who, for years, didn't even attend meetings. I am now a person who rarely misses any meeting because my perspective has changed. The Light of Masonry has been allowed to enter and uplift my soul. So for anyone reading this, I pray that if you have not yet made this journey, consider making that step to become one of us.

For those who have made the step, allow the Light of Masonry to move you to become a better Mason. If the first three degrees don't change you, then maybe this isn't the journey for you. No matter how many degrees you obtain, if it doesn't move you from darkness to light then it either wasn't done correctly or it never really touched your heart. Allow Freemasonry to make a change in you and, I pray, that you will feel as I do about the world's oldest fraternity.

Furthermore, as you read the ritual and the by-laws, it should give you a better sense of who and what we are and why we say that we take a good man and make him better. Realize this is done one man at a time which makes the whole significantly better. When we live ourselves beyond the rituals and by-laws in our Lodge Halls and extend charity, that's when we really embrace becoming a person who has come to the sublime degree of a Master Mason. This is where we all should be.

All of these things and more have opened my eyes. This is not to say that when I was a Master Mason in my Ancient Free and Accepted Lodge that I could not have come to knowledge in Masonry. But, it is to say that as a Black Man in America, becoming a Prince Hall Mason has attached our heritage to my Masonic experience. This is probably why I have grown in the art.

How do I now bring this Light to those who learn from me? I start by letting them know who Prince Hall was and what he did and what has come forth from him. This provides a good understanding of what it means to be a Prince Hall Mason. Then understanding what you went through and how you should use it in your life extends it. Not having this understanding initially, I believe, is another reason why I was just a Lodge Mason instead of a Master Mason. So I hope that my experience can bring that light to those who learn from me.

As we know, Freemasonry is a progressive science that must be learned. So we are given light a little at a time so that we can absorb it. Then, as we gain more light, we progress. If all the degrees are gained, there is still more learning to do. We never stop learning, so we should never stop teaching.

One statement that has changed the life of those who have come before me, can change the lives of those who are coming in now, and can change the lives of those who will come in in the future is "darkness to light." It has changed me, hopefully, for the better because I believe I have moved from darkness to light and have truly become a Master Mason. This is what Freemasonry means to me.

Masonry and Progress

Most Worshipful Brother
Ashby B. Carter
Grand Master
Prince Hall Grand Lodge of Illinois
1945 – 1953
Mt. Hebron Lodge #29

By saying that the objective of Freemasonry is to "put more Masonry in Men Rather than More Men in Masonry" is another way of saying that Masonry is a "progressive science." The supreme task of the craft is to labor unceasingly to improve society. We do this by searching always for Truth and then, finding it, we apply it unhesitatingly to all of our thoughts, words and deeds.

Acceptance of this principle plus the application of it to our daily activities spells progress. All of our ritual – our degree work, our lectures, our symbols, and our famed legends – point unerringly in this direction. Lazy Masons hear the words and witness the beautiful work and say, "Ah! I am a Mason." Industrious Masons know better the meaning of the words, symbols and allegories. They go beyond the ritual and seek the real story. They recognize the highly important fact that Masonry is a life of progressive advancement along the highway called "Truth".

Real Masons apply their ever-increasing knowledge to everyday, practical situations. For instance, they look about them and see the schools for which they pay taxes mishandled by seekers of spoils, causing their children to be robbed of their rightful opportunities for a sound education. They recognize the truth and set about to remedy the evil. Again, they see some men denied the right to occupations that their ability calls for solely because their skins are dark. They recognize the truth and labor for fair employment practice legislation. They see a whole people suffer because of a denial of civil rights, because of lynchings, poll taxes and Jim-Crow. They know the truth and join forces with agencies and people working for the elimination of these pernicious evils.

Do you find references to these things in the ritual? No, not specific terminology but they are there. Real Masons send their interests far beyond their immediate families. They send them out into the community, into the state, throughout the nation and throughout the world. The outcast in India, the exploited natives of Africa, the overburdened coolies of China, the victimized colonials of the world – all command the active interest of Real Masons. Are we not devotees of the Truth and faithful believers in the brotherhood of Man? Are we not our brothers' keepers?

Yes, I know all of the grips, signs and passwords. I wear as big a pin as any other Mason on earth. BUT, unless I can search my inner self and find there the constant, ever-present urge to accept the challenge that has come down through the generations to legions of brothers, I AM NOT a Mason except in name only. Real Masonry and progress are synonymous. Have I more Masonry in me today than I had yesterday? If I can answer in the affirmative, I am making genuine progress and I can Say in truth that I am a Mason!

Brother, are you a Mason?

Source: *Carter, Ashby B., "Masonry and Progress", Past Masters Topics, Vol. 1, Issue 1, Past Masters Council, 1946, p.1*

About Grand Master Carter

Ashby B. Carter, the twentieth Grand Master of Illinois Prince Hall Masons from 1945 to 1953, is considered by some to be one of the most prominent Prince Hall Masons of the twenty first century. While serving as Grand Master, he also served as President of the National Alliance of Postal Employees. Carter's efforts were extensive in fighting vigorous battles to secure the rights of African American federal employees. These efforts often found him conferring with Presidents of the United States of America including Harry S. Truman and Dwight D. Eisenhower for the cause. The results of these battles produced legislation to ensure equitable treatment under the law for all.

What Freemasonry Means to Me

Power

to Unite

Brother Eric Harrell
Cornerstone Lodge #91

Prior to 2010, I had no particular interest in a Masonic membership. I was approaching my 40th birthday, and had grown, somewhat, into a homebody. It was becoming my habit to just hang in my house. I was growing comfortable with it too. But seemingly from out nowhere, there came a strong urge in me to become a Mason. Or maybe it was just an urge to get up and out of the house and find something to do with my life besides go to work and occupy the house.

I'm a born and bred Chicago kind of guy. Over the years, I had frequented many places around Chicago. I would notice guys who I'd call, "those Masons". There was nothing implied in it. It was just the way I saw them. They were "those Masons" to me, and there was always "those Masons" in just about every place.

Everybody recognizes the Masonic emblem. Even still, there's a certain air that identifies Masons in a room. These men seemed set apart from others. I almost want to say, they seemed structured. The Masons appeared to my eyes as a type of Brotherhood, a cool and fun Brotherhood, enjoying life together as civil and peaceable adult men.

This was the observation about Masons that stuck with me. There was something to being a Mason. However, I was not ready to give it a try for a long time or not, at least, until I began to slow down in life. But upon my maturity, I thought of these men. I remembered. I wanted in on becoming part of the Brotherhood.

I began to show my active interest in joining the Brotherhood in the Fall of 2010. My first attempt though was with a Bogus Masonic Lodge. I was driving down South Ashland Avenue, and when I'd come to 55th, I saw the doors open to the Masonic Hall there. I drove around to park my car. I knocked on the door and was let in rather politely. When asked the reason for the visit, I stated to a gentlemen that I was interested in becoming a Freemason. We began to talk about a few introductory things. After not too long, I gave this guy my phone number. I'd say that I received a call around a few weeks later which led to my spending time with his lodge. It wasn't too long afterwards that I was given a petition. Thus my journey in Masonry began.

Today, I can happily say that my decision to join this Ancient Society of Honorable Men has been a rewarding one. I was healed into a Prince Hall Lodge in 2013, Cornerstone Lodge No. 91, and I've come to find that the idea and practice of Brotherhood really does exist in this organization. Although surely, it's a given, that no human institution is perfect. Masonry is no exception. That's just real life. But one thing for certain in my experience is that outside of church, I haven't found anything besides Masonry that binds me closer to my fellow man.

Thanks to Masonry, I have Brothers worldwide, and many new friendships locally as well. Masonry has put me in touch with some really good guys both near and far. This is the beauty of it to me. Masonry has real power to bring men together like no other organization.

Teaches Men

How to Live

Most Worshipful Brother
James H. Black Sr.
Grand Master
Prince Hall Grand Lodge of Illinois
1975 – 1977
Mt. Hebron Lodge #29

The real objective of Masonry is to teach men how to live. It effaces from among men the prejudice of case, the conventional distinction of color, origin, opinion, nationality and annihilates fanaticism and superstition. It exterminates national discord and, with it, extinguishes the firebrands of war, binding the people of all nations and all societies together by the bonds of science, morality, virtue and brotherly love.

Through the research of Freemasonry, I find that its good principles stand for humanity, and should be supported by every goo Mason; for Masonry has been of inestimable value in cementing worthy ties and strengthening good causes for hundreds of years. Because it does no deal in ordinary brands of publicity, and it many benevolences escape notice, it deserves special mention. The tenets of Freemasonry are best exemplified by the practices and conduct of every true Mason.

From time to time, legend dates Masonry back to King Solomon's Temple, and history traces its development within the First Century after the birth of Christ. At any rate, it is very ancient and has endured a vast deal of opposition and persecution without losing a particle of prestige.

Historians tell of the founders of the craft, who were skilled stonecutters and builders of the age when man's best art and artisanship were creating beautiful churches and cathedrals. The Masons were a chosen and selected body of men who followed their calling in wildly scattered towns and cities and who kept in constant touch with each other by secret signs and symbols which are used to this day.

The institution of Freemasonry is universal. It stretches from east to west, from north to south, and embraces within itself the representatives of every branch of the human family. It's carefully tiled doors swing open, not at the knock of every man, but at the demand of every true and worthy man duly accepted, whatever his religion, his race or his country be.

The Most Worshipful Prince Hall Grand Lodge of Illinois stands upon the high vantage ground of this American Society and recognizes the great principles which must necessarily underlie an institution which has a home on the continents and on the islands of the sea. The wisdom of Masonry is exemplified in establishing its basis on the immutable foundation of Truth. The shackles fell from the hands of prejudice and bigotry at the entrance of its shrine.

In its sacred retreat every discordant voice is hushed, and the bitterness of sectarian strife is abashed into silence in the awful presence of pure and absolute Truth. On any platform other than this, it could not comprehend in its embrace all tribes of men of the human race now existing or which have ever existed.

It is the recognition of these principles and the acknowledgement of corresponding obligations which along render it possible to make its privileges available to the whole of the great human family.

If Masonry should require any other creed than, that God is our Father, and that men are his children, and therefore bound to love Him and one another, its grand object would at once be defeated.

The mission of Freemasonry is to curb intemperate passion and to reconcile conflicting interests; to expand to nations of men those principles of humanity and benevolence which should actuate individuals to destroy the pride of conquest and the pomp of war; to annihilate local prejudice, and unreasonable partialities; to banish from the world every source of enmity and hostility, and to introduce those social feelings which are better calculated to preserve the peace and good order, than penal laws and political regulations.

I believe that every Mason should believe in and practice charity. For charities of men have existed in some shape or form, during every period of the world's history. Doubtless in the primitive ages, it became apparent that mutual protection would afford the greatest security against the unbroken forces of nature and the evil nature of men, and it secured sympathy, support and protection to those whose bond of union was made a common cause. Hence originated Masonry.

The advantages, which mankind in general reap from this master science, are beyond calculation. Its blessings are confined to no country but are diffused with the institutions throughout the world. Men of all languages, of all religions of the remotest nations and of every habit and opinion are united in a bond of brotherly love and affection.

Now, I believe that it is our mission as men and Masons to labor to restore this heretofore rejected, yet, underlying, stone of our institution of brotherly love.

Masonry has been the world's teacher of tolerance. The spirit of Masonry is the Gulf Stream that warms and tempers the current of modern civilization by relieving human suffering and eliminating class distinction, superstition and falsehood. It inspires men always to try to live and move on the plane of the square and level, under the law of love.

Widely though the problems of today differ from the problems sent for solution to Washington when he founded this nation, to Prince Hall when he founded this great fraternity of ours, and to Lincoln when he saves that nation and freed the slaves, yet, the qualities they showed in meeting these problems are exactly the same as those we should show in doing our work today.

My brethren, let's be about the business of carrying out the tenets of Masonry by building the character of men and not destroying the same.

Source: Black Sr., James H., "The Real Objective of Freemasonry", Prince Hall Masonic Journal, October 1975, MWPHGL of Illinois, p.6

About Grand Master Black

James H. Black Sr., the twenty ninth Grand Master of Illinois Prince Hall Masons from 1975 to 1977, is, by profession an accountant and one of the most respected Prince Hall Masons across the United States of America. He a man of God and is the pre-eminent teacher and scholar on Masonic jurisprudence. He not only holds the distinction of being the Senior-Most Past Grand Master of the Illinois jurisdiction but also the Senior-Most Deacon at Haven of Rest Baptist Church in Chicago, Illinois.